EARLY NETHERLANDISH PAINTING

ITS ORIGINS AND CHARACTER

The Charles Eliot Norton Lectures
1947–1948

EARLY

NETHERLANDISH

PAINTING

ITS ORIGINS AND CHARACTER

BY

Erwin Panofsky

VOLUME TWO

ICON EDITIONS

1817

HARPER & ROW, PUBLISHERS, New York

Cambridge, Philadelphia, San Francisco,
London, Mexico City, São Paulo, Sydney

This book was originally published by Harvard University Press. First Icon
edition published 1971.

STANDARD BOOK NUMBER: 06—436683-9

LIBRARY OF CONGRESS CATALOG CARD NUMBER: 52-5402

87 88 89 90 91   12 11 10 9

LIST OF ILLUSTRATIONS IN VOLUME TWO

ILLUSTRATIONS

vi

ILLUSTRATIONS

ILLUSTRATIONS

ILLUSTRATIONS

ILLUSTRATIONS

ILLUSTRATIONS

ILLUSTRATIONS

ILLUSTRATIONS

ILLUSTRATIONS

ILLUSTRATIONS

ILLUSTRATIONS

ILLUSTRATIONS

ILLUSTRATIONS

ILLUSTRATIONS

ILLUSTRATIONS

ILLUSTRATIONS

ILLUSTRATIONS

ILLUSTRATIONS

PLATES

2. Story of David; Paris, Bib. Nat, ms. lat. 1023.

1. Crucifixion; New York, Morgan Library, ms. 729.

Plate 1.

3. Philip the Fair and His Family; Paris, Bib. Nat., ms. lat. 8504.

4. Job, His Wife and a Friend; Paris, Bib. de l'Arsenal, ms. 5059.

Plate 2.

5. Annunciation; Paris, Rothschild Coll., Hours of Jeanne d'Evreux. 6. Duccio, Annunciation of the Virgin's Death; Siena, Opera del Duomo.
7. Lamentation; Paris, Rothschild Coll., Hours of Jeanne d'Evreux. 8. Duccio, Lamentation; Siena, Opera del Duomo.

Plate 3.

10. Illuminated Page; Paris, Bib. Nat, ms. lat. 10483.

9. Illuminated Page; Verdun, Bib. Municipale, ms. 107.

Plate 4.

12. January; Paris, Bib. Nat, ms. lat. 10484.

11. December; Paris, Bib. Nat, ms. lat. 10483.

Plate 5.

13. February; Paris, Rothschild Coll.

14. March; Paris, Rothschild Coll.

15. February; Hours of Bonne of Luxembourg
(Location Unknown).

16. March; Paris, Bib. Nat., ms, lat. 18014.

Plate 6.

17. Dedication Miniature; Paris, Bib. Nat., ms. fr. 1950. 18. Blanche of Burgundy Adoring the Trinity; Portsmouth, Cath. Episc. Library, *Heures de Savoie.* 19. St Leonard; *ibidem.*
20. Christ Healing the Palsied Man; The Hague, Mus. Meermanno-Westreenianum, ms. 10 B 23. 21. David and Goliath; *ibidem.*
22. Nativity; The Hague, Mus. Meermanno-Westreenianum, ms. 10 A 14.

Plate 7.

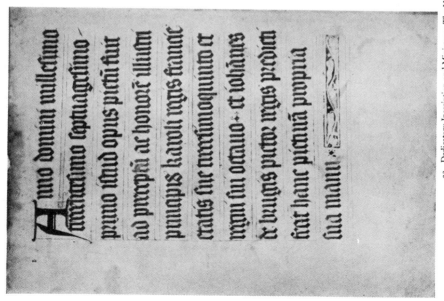

23. Dedicatory Inscription and Miniature; The Hague, Mus. Meermanno-Westreenianum, ms. 10 B 23.

Plate 8.

24. Lot and His Daughters; Paris, Bib. Nat., ms. fr. 15397.

25. Revelation XIV, 13 (Tapestry); Angers, Musée des Tapisseries.

Plate 9.

27. St. John the Evangelist; Paris, Bib. Nat., ms. fr. 13091.

26. David; Paris, Bib. Nat., ms. fr. 13091.

Plate 10.

28. Jean le Bon; Paris, Louvre.

Plate 11.

29. *Parement de Narbonne, Central Section; Paris, Louvre.*

Plate 12.

31. Baptism of Christ (Enlarged); Paris, Bib. Nat, ms. lat. 18014.

30. Matins Page (Reduced); Paris, Bib. Nat, ms. lat. 18014.

Plate 13.

35.

36.

34.

32.

33.

Plate 14.

38. Pisan Master, Nativity; Pisa, Museo Civico.

37. Nativity; Turin, Museo Civico, *Très-Belles Heures*.

Plate 15.

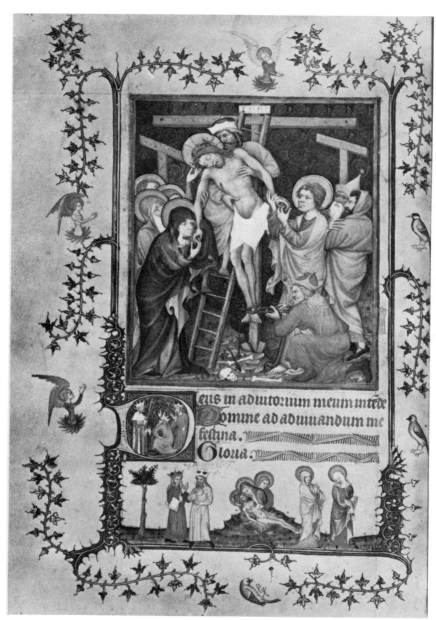

39. Descent from the Cross and Lamentation; Paris, Rothschild Collection, *Très-Belles Heures*.

Plate 16.

40. First Dedication Page; Brussels, Bib. Royale, ms. 11060/61.

Plate 17.

42. Annunciation; Brussels, Bib. Royale, ms. 11060/61.

41. Second Dedication Page; Brussels, Bib. Royale, ms. 11060/61.

Plate 18.

44. Flight into Egypt; Brussels, Bib. Royale, ms. 11060/61.

43. Visitation; Brussels, Bib. Royale, ms. 11060/61.

Plate 19.

46. Simone Martini, Bearing of the Cross; Paris, Louvre.

186.

45. Bearing of the Cross; Brussels, Bib. Royale, ms. 11060/61.

Plate 20.

47. Illuminated Page; Paris, Bib. Nat., ms. lat. 919.

Plate 21.

Plate 22.

Ey apres deuile du chien doyfel er de toute fa nature.

50. The Bird Hound; Paris, Bib. de l'Arsenal, ms. 616.

a cour et la contree ou les tritats demourui

51. The Land of the Tartars; Paris, Bib. Nat., ms. fr. 12201.

Plate 23.

52. Crucifixion; Brussels, Bib. Royale, ms. 9125.

Plate 24.

53. Penthesilea; Paris, Bib. Nat., ms. fr. 598.

56. *Caritas Romana*; Paris, Bib. Nat., ms. fr. 598.

55. Sappho; Paris, Bib. Nat., ms. fr. 598.

54. Antiope and Oreithyia; Paris, Bib. Nat., ms. fr. 12420.

Plate 25.

57. Creation of Adam; Paris, Bib. de l'Arsenal, ms. 5057.

58. Judgment and Parables of Solomon; Paris, Bib. de l'Arsenal, ms. 5058.

Plate 26.

59. Visitation; Paris, Mus. Jacquemart-André, Boucicaut Hours.

Plate 27.

61. St. Jerome; Paris, Mus. Jacquemart-André, Boucicaut Hours.

60. Annunciation; Paris, Mus. Jacquemart-André, Boucicaut Hours.

Plate 28.

63. Coronation of the Virgin; Paris, Mus. Jacquemart-André, Boucicaut Hours.

62. Vigils of the Dead; Paris, Mus. Jacquemart-André, Boucicaut Hours.

Plate 29.

Plate 30.

67. Adoration of the Magi; Paris, Mus. Jacquemart-André, Boucicaut Hours.

66. Nativity; Paris, Mus. Jacquemart-André, Boucicaut Hours.

Plate 31.

69. Charles VI and Pierre Salmon; Geneva, Bib. Publique et Universitaire, ms. fr. 165.

68. Scene from *Dialogues* of Pierre Salmon; Paris, Bib. Nat, ms. fr. 23279.

Plate 32.

70. Vigils of the Dead; Paris, Bib. Nat.,
ms. lat. 10538.

71. Birth of St. John; Bourges, Bib. de la Ville,
ms. 34.

72. Nativity; Paris, Bib. Nat.,
ms. lat. 10538.

73. Nativity; Baltimore, Walters Art Gallery,
ms. 260.

Plate 33.

74. Annunciation; Paris, Bib. Nat., ms. lat. 1161.

75. *Piété Nostre Seigneur*; Paris, Bib. Nat., ms. lat. 1161.

76. Funeral Service; Paris, Bib. Nat., ms. lat. 1161.

77. Journey of the Magi; Paris, Bib. Nat., ms. fr. 2810.

Plate 34.

78. Donatrix Venerating the Madonna; Paris, Bib. Nat., ms. lat. 1161.

79. Coronation of Hannibal; Paris, Bib. Nat., ms. fr. 259.

Plate 35.

80. Annunciation; Chantilly, Mus. Condé, *Très Riches Heures*.

Plate 36.

82. Fall of Man and Expulsion from Paradise; Chantilly, Mus. Condé, *Très Riches Heures.*

81. Nativity and Annunciation to the Shepherds; Chantilly, Mus. Condé, *Très Riches Heures.*

Plate 37.

Plate 38.

85. Constantine (Medal);
Vienna, Kunsthistorisches Museum.

86. Giotto, Stigmatization of St. Francis; Florence, Santa Croce.

Plate 39.

87. Christ at Gethsemane; Chantilly, Mus. Condé, *Très Riches Heures*.

Plate 40.

89. February; Chantilly, Mus. Condé, *Très Riches Heures.*

88. January; Chantilly, Mus. Condé, *Très Riches Heures.*

Plate 41.

91. April; Chantilly, Mus. Condé, *Très Riches Heures.*

90. March; Chantilly, Mus. Condé, *Très Riches Heures.*

Plate 42.

92. Franco-Flemish Master of *ca.* 1420, Young Lady;
Washington, National Gallery.

93. Group of Ladies; Chantilly, Mus. Condé,
Très Riches Heures.

94. April Master of the *Très Riches Heures*, John the
Fearless (Copy); Paris, Louvre.

95. Detail of fig. 91. Chantilly, Mus. Condé,
Très Riches Heures.

Plate 43.

mater dei. J ctrsa
lue maria. Aqui
dieu sonfilz man a

96. Madonna; Cambridge, Mass., Harvard University Library, De Buz Hours.

Plate 44.

98. Dying Man Commending His Soul to God; Paris, Bib. Nat., ms. lat. 9471.

97. Annunciation to the Shepherds; Paris, Bib. Nat., ms. lat. 9471.

Plate 45.

99. Valencian Master of *ca.* 1420, the "Carrand Diptych"; Florence, Museo Nazionale.

Plate 46.

100. Jean Malouel and Henri Bellechose, Martyrdom of St. Denis; Paris, Louvre.

Plate 47.

101. Jean Malouel, Trinity with the Virgin and St. John the Evangelist;
Paris, Louvre.

102. French Master of *ca.* 1410, Coronation of the Virgin; Berlin,
Kaiser Friedrich Museum.

Plate 48.

103. Utrecht Master of 1363, Calvary of Hendrik van Rijn; Antwerp, Musée Royal.

Plate 49.

104. Melchior Broederlam, Annunciation and Visitation; Dijon, Musée de la Ville.

Plate 50.

105. Melchior Broederlam, Presentation of Christ and Flight into Egypt; Dijon, Musée de la Ville.

Plate 51.

106. Mosan Master of *ca.* 1415, Triptych, Exterior; Vierhouten, van Beuningen Coll.

Plate 52.

107. Mosan Master of *ca.* 1415, Triptych, Interior; Vierhouten, van Beuningen Coll.

Plate 53.

108 a.

108 b.

108 c.

108. Guelders(?) Master of 1400–1410, Quadriptych, Left Half; *a.* and *b.* Baltimore,
Walters Art Gallery; *c.* Antwerp, Musée Mayer van den Bergh.

Plate 54.

109 a.

109 b.

109 c.

109. Guelders (?) Master of 1400–1410, Quadriptych, Right Half; *a.* and *c.* Antwerp,
Musée Mayer van den Bergh; *b.* Baltimore, Walters Art Gallery.

Plate 55.

Plate 56.

112. Brabantine Master of *ca.* 1400, Birth of the Virgin; Brussels, Musée Royal.

113. Bruges Master of *ca.* 1400, Calvary of the Tanners: Bruges, St.-Sauveur.

Plate 57.

115. Creation of the World; Baltimore, Walters Art Gallery, ms. 171.

119. Madonna; London, Brit. Mus., ms. Add. 38527.

116. Emperor, Knight and Husbandman; New York, Morgan Library, ms. 691.

117. Christ in the Winepress; London, Brit. Mus., ms. Add. 22288.

114. Alexander the Great on His Deathbed; Brussels, Bib. Royale, ms. 205 A.

118. Last Judgment; Baltimore, Walters Art Gallery, ms. 185.

Plate 58.

120. Mary, Duchess of Guelders, and Betrayal of Christ; Berlin, Staatsbibliothek, Cod. germ. 4° 42.

Plate 59.

Plate 60.

121. The *Salvator Mundi*; New York, Morgan Library, ms. 87

122. David's Victory over Goliath; *ibidem.*

123. The Brazen Serpent; New York,
Morgan Library, ms. 87.

124. St. John the Baptist Preaching;
ibidem.

125. The Prophet Jonah;
ibidem.

126. Coronation of the
Virgin; *ibidem.*

Plate 61.

127. Nativity; Formerly Kottbus, Bum Collection, Book of Hours.

128. Adoration of the Magi; The Hague, Mus. Meermanno-Westreenianum, ms. 10 E 1.

129. Crucifixion; Nordkirchen, Duke of Arenberg, Book of Hours.

130. Descent from the Cross; Nordkirchen, Duke of Arenberg, Book of Hours.

Plate 62.

131. Annunciation; Liége, Bib. Universitaire, ms. 35.

132. Nativity; *ibidem.*

133. Chorus of Angels; London, Brit. Mus.,
ms. Egerton 859.

134. Susanna and the Elders;
ibidem.

Plate 63.

135. Saturn in His Mansions; New York, Morgan Library, ms. 785.

Plate 64.

137. The Moon in Exaltation; New York, Morgan Library, ms. 785.

136. Mercury in Exaltation; New York, Morgan Library, ms. 785.

Plate 65.

141. The Sermon on the Mount; Brussels, Bib. Royale, ms. 11041.

138. The Pilgrim meeting Envy; Brussels, Bib. Royale, ms. 10176/78.

139. Five Wicked Jews; Wiesbaden, Staatsarchiv.

140. Equity and Felony; Brussels, Bib. Royale, ms. 11041.

Plate 66.

147. Last Supper; Brussels, Bib. Royale, ms. II, 7831.

1.8. Chr.st Appearing to His Mother; *ibidem*.

149. Dedication Page; Tournai, Bib. Municipale, ms. 42.

145. Annunciation; Paris, Bib. Nat., ms. lat. 1364.

146. Baptism of Christ; Paris, Bib. Nat., ms, lat. 1364.

142. Annunciation; Brussels, Bib. Royale, ms. II, 7831.

143. Nativity; *ibidem*.

144. Entry into Jerusalem; *ibidem*.

Plate 67.

150. Revelation I; Paris, Bib. Nat., ms. néerl. 3.

Plate 68.

152. Revelation VIII; Paris, Bib. Nat., ms. néerl. 3.

151. Revelation II, III; Paris, Bib. Nat, ms. néerl. 3.

Plate 69.

153. Liége (?) Master of *ca.* 1400, Triptych; Berlin, Deutsches Museum.

Plate 70.

155. Flight into Egypt; Rouen, Bib. de la Ville, ms. 3024.

154. Dedication Page; Rouen, Bib. de la Ville, ms. 3024.

Plate 71.

157. Nativity; Rouen, Bib. de la Ville, ms. 3024.

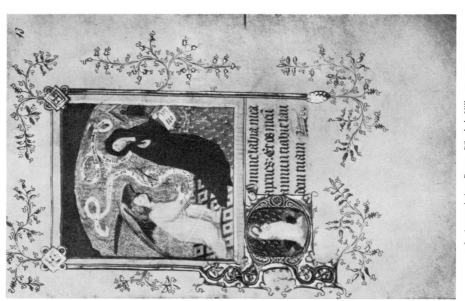

156. Annunciation; Rouen, Bib. de la Ville, ms. 3024.

Plate 72.

159. The Madonna, St. Catherine and St. Agnes in the Garden of Paradise;
Carpentras, Bib. de la Ville, ms. 57.

158. The Holy Face and the Garden of Paradise;
Rouen, Bib. de la Ville, ms. 3024

Plate 73.

161. Annunciation; Frankfort-on-the-Main, Museum für Kunsthandwerk, ms. Linel 11.

160. St. Bernard; Frankfort-on-the-Main, Muesum für Kunsthandwerk, ms. Linel 11.

Plate 74.

165. Annunciation; Indianapolis, Dr. Clowes Coll., Book of Hours.

162. St. Christopher; Oxford, Bodleian Library, ms. Can. Lit. 118.

164. Melchior Broederlam; Detail of fig. 104

163. St. Christopher; Carpentras, Bib. de la Ville, ms. 57.

Plate 75.

170

171

172

169

166. Immaculate Conception; London, Brit. Mus., ms. Add. 29704.
167. St. Louis; *ibidem.*
168. St. John the Evangelist; London, Brit. Mus., ms. Add. 16998.
169. Story of St. Martin; London, Brit. Mus., ms. Add. 29704.
170. Annunciation; London, Brit. Mus., ms. Add. 16998.
171. Portrait of the Owner; *ibidem.*
172. Madonna of Humility; *ibidem.*

166

167

168

Plate 76.

174. Annunciation; London, Brit. Mus., ms. Royal 2 A XVIII.

173. St. Christopher; London, Brit. Mus., ms. Royal 2 A XVIII.

Plate 77.

175. Annunciation; London, Lambeth Palace Library, ms. 69.
177. Anointing of David; *ibidem.*   178. Entombment; *ibidem.*
180. Nativity; *ibidem.*

176. Annunciation; London, Brit. Mus., ms. Add. 42131.
179. Annunciation; London; Brit. Mus., ms. Add. 18213.

Plate 78.

181. English Master of *ca.* 1415, The Wilton Diptych; London, National Gallery.

Plate 79.

182. Nativity; Paris, Bib. Nat., ms. lat. Nouv. Acq. 3055.

183. St. Christopher; *ibidem*.

184. Derision of Christ; *ibidem*.

185. St. Andrew; *ibidem*.

Plate 80.

187. St. Christopher and St. Anthony;
Baltimore, Walters Art Gallery, ms. 166.

186. Daniel in the Lions' Den Venerated by Daniel Rym;
Baltimore, Walters Art Gallery, ms. 166.

Plate 81.

188. Bearing of the Cross; Baltimore,
Walters Art Gallery, ms. 166.

189. Betrayal of Christ; Baltimore, Walters
Art Gallery, ms. 166.

190. St. Barbara; Baltimore, Walters
Art Gallery, ms. 170.

191. Rest on the Flight into Egypt; Baltimore,
Walters Art Gallery, ms. 211.

Plate 82.

192. St. John the Baptist; New York, Morgan Library, ms. 439.

193. St. George; Providence, R. I., J. C. Brown Library, ms. 3.

194. St. George; Lisbon, National Archives, Duarte Hours.

195. St. George; Bruges, Grand Séminaire, ms. vol. 72/175.

Plate 83.

196. The Master of Flémalle; Triptych. The Entombment; The Resurrection; A Donor. London, Count A. Seilern Collection.

Plate 84.

Plate 85.

199. Master of Flémalle, Betrothal of the Virgin; Madrid, Prado.

Plate 86.

Plate 87.

201. Master of Flémalle, Nativity; Dijon, Musée de la Ville.

Plate 88.

202. Master of Flémalle; Detail of fig. 201.

Plate 89.

203. Master of Flémalle, Madonna; London, National Gallery.

Plate 90.

204. Master of Flémalle, The "Mérode Altarpiece"; Formerly Westerloo-Tongerloo, Princess de Mérode.

Plate 91.

205. Master of Flémalle, The Bad Thief; Frankfort-on-the-Main, Städelsches Kunstinstitut.

Plate 92.

208. Master of Flémalle, St. Veronica; Frankfort-on-the-Main, Städelsches Kunstinstitut.

207. Master of Flémalle, Trinity; Frankfort-on-the-Main, Städelsches Kunstinstitut.

206. Master of Flémalle, Madonna; Frankfort-on-the-Main, Städelsches Kunstinstitut.

Plate 93.

209. Master of Flémalle, Madonna in a Glory; Aix-en-Provence,
Mus. Granet.

Plate 94.

210. Master of Flémalle, Trinity; Leningrad, Hermitage.

Plate 95.

211. Master of Flémalle, Madonna at the Fireplace; Leningrad, Hermitage.

Plate 96.

212. Master of Flémalle, The Werl Altarpiece,
Left Wing; Madrid, Prado.

213. Master of Flémalle, The Werl Altarpiece,
Right Wing; Madrid, Prado.

Plate 97.

215. Roger van der Weyden, Detail of fig. 310.

214. Master of Flémalle, Detail of fig. 213.

Plate 98.

216. Master of Flémalle, Christ and the Virgin Mary; Philadelphia, Pennsylvania Museum of Art, Johnson Coll.

Plate 99.

217. Master of Flémalle, Portrait of a Gentleman; London, National Gallery.

Plate 100.

218. Master of Flémalle, Portrait of a Lady; London, National Gallery.

Plate 101.

219. Master of Flémalle (?), Portrait of a Musician; New York, Mrs. J. Magnin Coll.

Plate 102.

Plate 103.

222. Master of Flémalle, Madonna in an Apse
(Copy); New York, Metropolitan Museum.

223. Master of Flémalle, Adoration of the Magi
(Copy); Berlin, Kaiser Friedrich Museum.

224. Master of Flémalle, Vengeance of Tomyris (Copy); Berlin,
Kaiser Friedrich Museum.

225. Master of Flémalle, Jael Slaying Sisera (Pen,
Copy); Braunschweig, Landesmuseum.

Plate 104.

226. Master of Flémalle Madonna of Humility
(Copy); Brussels, G. Müller Coll.

227. Master of Flémalle, Mass of St. Gregory (Copy);
New York, E. Schwarz Coll.

228. Colin de Coter (Probably after the Master of
Flémalle), St. Luke Painting the Virgin;
Vieure, Church.

229. Gerard David (after the Master of
Flémalle), Crucifixion; Lugano,
Thyssen Coll.

Plate 105.

230. Master of Flémalle Triptych (Copy); Liverpool, Walker Art Gallery.

Plate 106.

Plate 107.

232. Jacques Daret, Visitation; Berlin, Kaiser Friedrich
Museum.

233. Jacques Daret, Nativity; Lugano,
Thyssen Coll.

234. Jacques Daret, Adoration of the Magi; Berlin,
Kaiser Friedrich Museum.

235. Jacques Daret, Presentation of Christ; Paris,
Petit Palais.

Plate 108.

236. Jan van Eyck, Madonna in a Church; Berlin,
Kaiser Friedrich Museum.

Plate 109.

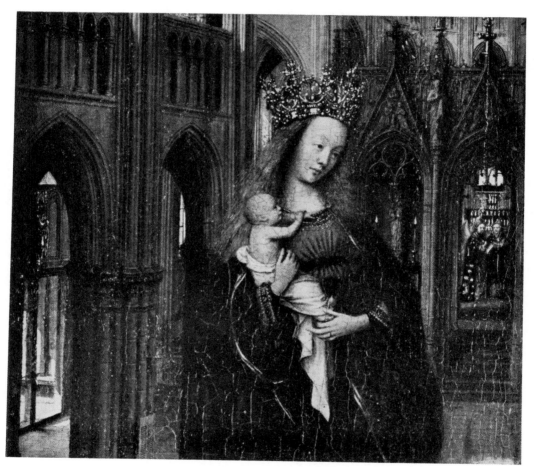

237. Jan van Eyck; Detail of fig. 236.

Plate 110.

238. Jan van Eyck, Annunciation; Washington,
National Gallery.

Plate III.

239. Jan van Eyck; Detail of fig. 238.

Plate 112.

240. Jan van Eyck, Triptych; Dresden, Gemäldegalerie.

Plate 113.

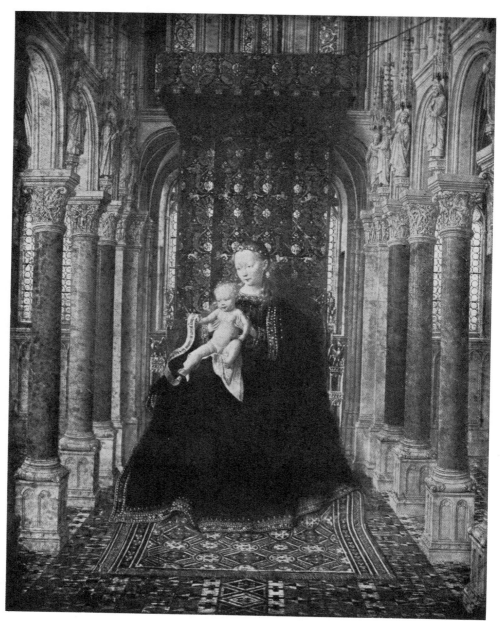

241. Jan van Eyck, Madonna; Central Panel of fig. 240.

Plate 114.

242. Jan van Eyck Annunciation; Exterior Wings of fig. 240.

Plate 115.

243. Jan van Eyck, Madonna; Melbourne, National Gallery.

Plate 116.

244. Jan van Eyck, Madonna of Chancellor Rolin; Paris, Louvre.

Plate 117.

245. Jan van Eyck; Detail of fig. 244.

Plate 118.

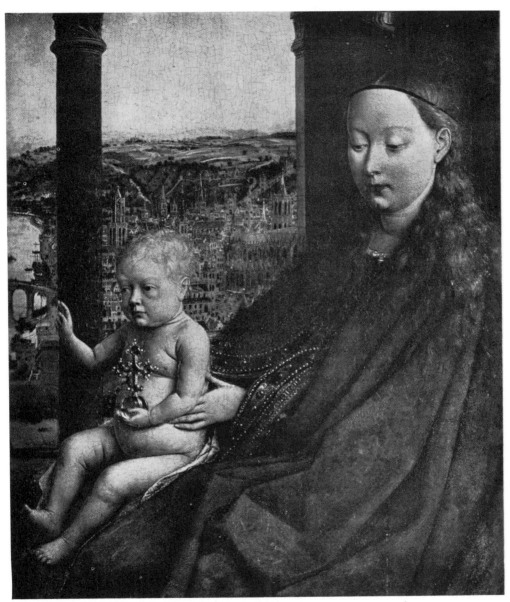

246. Jan van Eyck; Detail of fig. 244.

Plate 119.

247. Jan van Eyck, Giovanni Arnolfini and Jeanne Cenami; London, National Gallery.

Plate 120.

248. Jan van Eyck, Madonna of Canon George van der Paele; Bruges, Musée Communal.

Plate 121.

249. Jan van Eyck; Detail of fig. 248.

250. Master of Flémalle; Detail of fig. 205.

251. Roger van der Weyden; Detail of fig. 314.

Plate 122.

252. Jan van Eyck, the "Lucca Madonna"; Frankfort, Städelsches Kunstinstitut.

Plate 123.

253. Jan van Eyck, Annunciation; Lugano, Thyssen Coll.

Plate 124.

254. Jan van Eyck, St. Barbara; Antwerp, Musée Royal.

Plate 125.

255. Jan van Eyck, Madonna at the Fountain; Antwerp, Musée Royal.

Plate 126.

256. Jan van Eyck (?), The Holy Face; Durham, J. C. Swinborne Coll. (?).

Plate 127.

257. Jan van Eyck and Petrus Christus, Madonna of Jan Vos; Paris, Rothschild Coll.

Plate 128.

258. Jan van Eyck and Petrus Christus, St. Jerome; Detroit, Institute of Arts.

Plate 129.

Plate 130.

260. Jan van Eyck, Baudouin de Lannoy; Berlin, Kaiser Friedrich Museum.

Plate 131.

261. Jan van Eyck, "Timotheos" (Gilles Binchois?); London, National Gallery.

Plate 132.

262. Jan van Eyck, Man in a Red Turban; London, National Gallery.

Plate 133.

263. Jan van Eyck, Nicholas Cardinal Albergati; Vienna, Gemäldegalerie.

Plate 134.

264. Jan van Eyck, Nicholas Cardinal Albergati (Silverpoint); Formerly Dresden, Kupferstichkabinett.

Plate 135.

265. Jan van Eyck, The Goldsmith Jan de Leeuw; Vienna, Gemäldegalerie.

Plate 136.

266. Jan van Eyck, Giovanni Arnolfini; Berlin, Kaiser Friedrich Museum.

Plate 137.

267. Jan van Eyck, Margaret van Eyck; Bruges, Musée Communal.

Plate 138.

268. Follower of Jan van Eyck, Stigmatization of St. Francis; Philadelphia, Pennsylvania Museum of Art, Johnson Coll.

269. Follower of Jan van Eyck, Stigmatization of St. Francis; Turin, Galleria Sabauda.

Plate 139.

271. Imitator of Jan van Eyck, The Man with the Pink; Berlin, Kaiser Friedrich Museum.

270. Imitator of Jan van Eyck, Portrait of a Goldsmith; Sibiu, Bruckenthal Museum.

Plate 140.

273. Unidentified Artist, St. George; Formerly London, Lady E. Mason Coll.

272. Pedro Nisart after Jan van Eyck, St. George; Palma, Museo Arqueológico.

Plate 141.

274. Jan van Eyck, Ghent Altarpiece, Exterior; Ghent, St. Bavo's.

Plate 142.

275. Hubert and Jan van Eyck, Ghent Altarpiece, Interior; Ghent, St. Bavo's.

Plate 143.

276. Jan van Eyck, Annunciation; Detail of fig. 274.

Plate 144.

277. Jan van Eyck, The Two St. Johns and Donors; Detail of fig. 274.

Plate 145.

278. Hubert and Jan van Eyck, Adoration of the Lamb; Detail of fig. 275.

Plate 146.

279. Hubert and Jan van Eyck, Judges, Knights, Hermits and Pilgrims; Detail of fig. 275.

Plate 147.

280. Hubert and Jan van Eyck, The Virgin Mary, The Lord, St. John the Baptist; Detail of fig. 275.

Plate 148.

281. Jan van Eyck, Adam and Eve; Detail of fig. 275.

Plate 149.

282. Hubert and Jan van Eyck, Musical Angels; Detail of fig. 275.

Plate 150.

283 a. Jan van Eyck, Virgin Martyrs; Detail of fig. 278.

283 b. Hubert van Eyck, Apostles; Detail of fig. 278.

Plate 151.

284. Hubert van Eyck (?), Annunciation; New York, Metropolitan Museum.

Plate 152.

285. Hubert and Jan van Eyck (?), The Three Marys at the Tomb; Vierhouten, van Beuningen Coll.

Plate 153.

Plate 154.

288. Follower of Jan van Eyck, Agony in the Garden; Turin, Museo Civico, *Très-Belles Heures.*

287. Follower of Jan van Eyck, The Lord Enthroned; Formerly Turin, Royal Library, *Très-Belles Heures.*

Plate 155.

Plate 156.

292. Nicola di Maestro Antonio (?), Calvary; Venice, Accademia.

291. Unknown Flemish Master after Jan van Eyck, Calvary; Venice, Cà d'Oro.

Plate 157.

293. Follower of Jan van Eyck, Crucifixion; Berlin, Kaiser Friedrich Museum.

Plate 158.

Within the miniature:

mnes sancte uirgines mentis
et corporis puritatem.

294. Jan van Eyck, The Virgin Among Virgins; Formerly Turin, Royal Library, *Très-Belles Heures*.

Plate 159.

295. Jan van Eyck, Finding of the True Cross; Turin, Museo Civico, *Très-Belles Heures*.

Plate 160.

296. Jan van Eyck, St. Julian Ferrying Christ; Formerly Turin, Royal Library, *Très-Belles Heures*.

Plate 161.

297. Jan van Eyck, Prayer on the Shore; Formerly Turin, Royal Library, *Très-Belles Heures.*

Plate 162.

298. Jan van Eyck, Betrayal of Christ; Formerly Turin, Royal Library, *Très-Belles Heures*.

Plate 163.

c uentre matris mee uccauit me dñs
nomine meo. et posiut os meu sicut
gladium acutum subtegumento
manus sue protexit me posuit me

299. Jan van Eyck, Birth of St. John; Turin, Museo Civico, *Très-Belles Heures*.

Plate 164.

300. Jan van Eyck, Mass of the Dead; Turin, Museo Civico, *Très-Belles Heures*.

Plate 165.

301. Jan van Eyck, Diptych; New York, Metropolitan Museum.

Plate 166.

302. Copy after Jan van Eyck, Adoration of the Magi (Pen); Berlin, Kupferstichkabinett.

Plate 167.

303. Jan van Eyck, Details of fig. 301.

Plate 168.

304. Free Copy after Jan van Eyck, Bearing of the Cross (Pen); Vienna, Albertina.

305. Free Copy after Jan van Eyck, Bearing of the Cross; Budapest,
Museum of Fine Arts.

Plate 169.

306. Roger van der Weyden, Madonna Enthroned; Lugano, Thyssen Collection.

Plate 170.

308. Co-worker of Roger van der Weyden, St. Catherine; Vienna, Gemäldegalerie.

307. Roger van der Weyden, Madonna Standing; Vienna, Gemäldegalerie.

Plate 171.

309 a.

309 b.

309 c.

309. Roger van der Weyden and Follower, Triptych; Turin, Galleria Sabauda (a and c), and Paris, Louvre (b).

Plate 172.

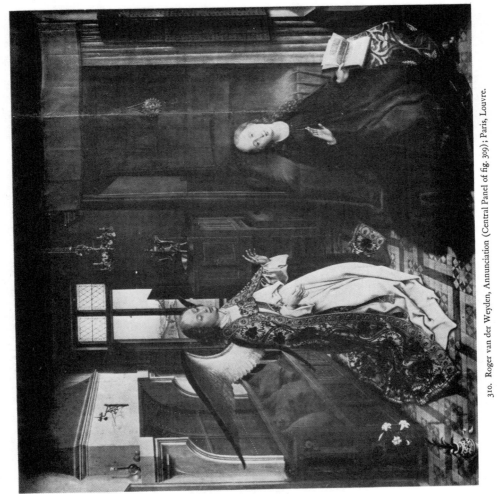

310. Roger van der Weyden, Annunciation (Central Panel of fig. 309); Paris, Louvre.

Plate 173.

312. Follower of Roger van der Weyden, Visitation (fig. 309 c); Turin, Galleria Sabauda.

311. Roger van der Weyden, Visitation; Lützschena, Speck von Sternburg Coll.

Plate 174.

313. Roger van der Weyden (?), St. Luke Painting the Virgin; Boston, Museum of Fine Arts.

Plate 175.

314. Roger van der Weyden, Descent from the Cross; Madrid, Prado.

Plate 176.

315. Roger van der Weyden; Details of fig. 314.

Plate 177.

316. Roger van der Weyden, The Magdalen (Fragment); London, National Gallery.

Plate 178.

317. Roger van der Weyden, Madonna Enthroned; Madrid, Prado.

Plate 179.

318. Roger van der Weyden, The "Miraflores Altarpiece"; Berlin, Kaiser Friedrich Museum.

Plate 180.

319. Roger van der Weyden, Holy Family; Left Panel of fig. 318.

Plate 181.

320. Roger van der Weyden, Lamentation; Central Panel of fig. 318.

Plate 182.

321. Roger van der Weyden, Christ Appearing to His Mother; New York, Metropolitan Museum.

Plate 183.

322. Roger van der Weyden, Triptych; Vienna, Gemäldegalerie.

Plate 184.

323. Roger van der Weyden; Detail of fig. 322.

Plate 185.

324. Roger van der Weyden; Detail of fig. 322.

Plate 186.

325. Roger van der Weyden and Assistants, Last Judgment Altarpiece, Exterior; Beaune, Hôtel-Dieu.

Plate 187.

326. Roger van der Weyden, Last Judgment Altarpiece, Interior; Beaune, Hôtel-Dieu.

Plate 188.

327. Roger van der Weyden, The Judge and St. Michael; Detail of fig. 326.

Plate 189.

328. Roger van der Weyden; Detail of fig. 326.

Plate 190.

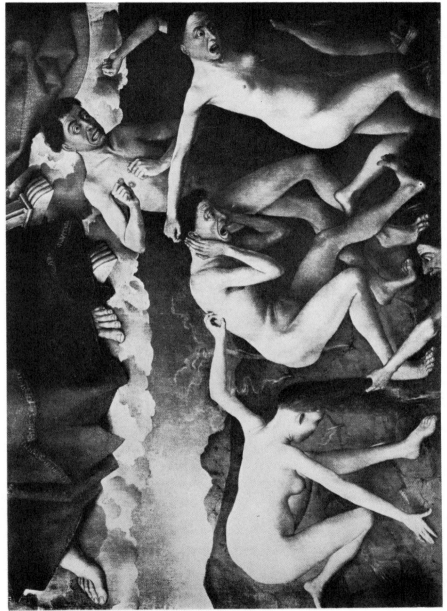

329. Roger van der Weyden; Detail of fig. 326.

Plate 191.

330. Dedication Page, Probably Designed by Roger van der Weyden; Brussels, Bib. Royale, ms. 9241.

Plate 192.

331. Roger van der Weyden, Entombment; Florence, Uffizi.

Plate 193.

332. Roger van der Weyden, Madonna and Saints; Frankfort, Städelsches Kunstinstitut.

Plate 194.

333. Roger van der Weyden, Triptych of Jean de Braque; Paris, Louvre.

Plate 195.

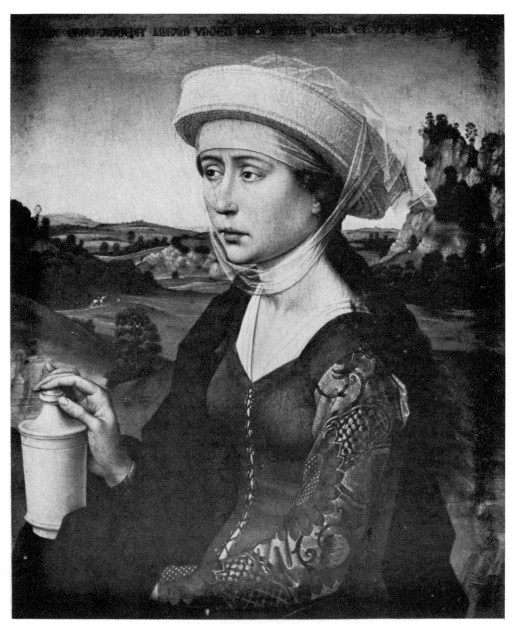

334. Roger van der Weyden, The Magdalen; Right Wing of fig. 333.

Plate 196.

335.

336.

335, 336. Roger van der Weyden and Assistant, The "Bladelin Altarpiece"; Berlin, Kaiser Friedrich Museum.

Plate 197.

337. **Roger van der Weyden, Nativity; Central Panel of fig. 336.**

Plate 198.

338. Roger van der Weyden, The Visions of Augustus (a) and the Three Magi (b); Wings of fig. 336.

Plate 199.

339. Roger van der Weyden; Detail of fig. 337.

Plate 200.

341. Roger van der Weyden, David Receiving the Cistern Water (fragment):
Formerly Paris, Schloss Coll.

340. Roger van der Weyden, Augustus and the Sibyl of Tibur;
Detail of fig. 338.

Plate 201.

342. Roger van der Weyden, The St. John Altarpiece; Berlin, Kaiser Friedrich Museum.

Plate 202.

343. Roger van der Weyden, Birth and Naming of St. John the Baptist; Left Panel of fig. 342.

Plate 203.

344. Roger van der Weyden, Baptism of Christ; Central Panel of fig. 342.

Plate 204.

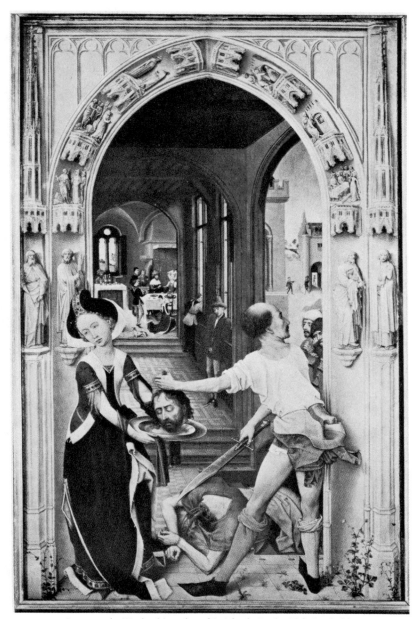

345. Roger van der Weyden, Martyrdom of St. John the Baptist; Right Panel of fig. 342.

Plate 205.

346. Roger van der Weyden; Detail of fig. 343.

Plate 206.

347. Roger van der Weyden (Executed by Assistant), Altarpiece of the Seven Sacraments; Antwerp, Mus. Royal.

Plate 207.

348. Roger van der Weyden (Executed by Assistant), The Eucharist;
Central Panel of fig. 347.

Plate 208.

349. Roger van der Weyden (Executed by Assistant), Six Sacraments; Wings of fig. 347.

Plate 209.

350. Roger van der Weyden, Calvary, Left Wing; Philadelphia,
Pennsylvania Museum of Art, Johnson Coll.

Plate 210.

351. Roger van der Weyden, Calvary, Right Wing; Philadelphia, Pennsylvania Museum of Art, Johnson Coll.

Plate 211.

352. Roger van der Weyden, The "Columba Altarpiece"; Munich, Alte Pinakothek.

Plate 212.

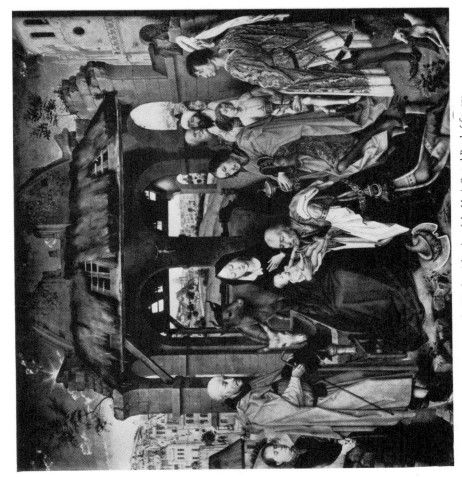

353. Roger van der Weyden, Adoration of the Magi; Central Panel of fig. 352.

Plate 213.

354. Roger van der Weyden, Annunciation and Presentation of Christ; Wings of fig. 352.

Plate 214.

355. Roger van der Weyden; Detail of fig. 353.

Plate 215.

356. Roger van der Weyden; Detail of fig. 353.

Plate 216.

357. Roger van der Weyden, Crucifixion; Escorial.

Plate 217.

358. Roger van der Weyden; Detail of fig. 357 before Restoration.

Plate 218.

359. Follower of Roger van der Weyden, Lamentation; The Hague, Mauritshuis.

Plate 219.

360. Roger van der Weyden, Portrait of a Young Lady; Berlin, Kaiser Friedrich Museum.

Plate 220.

362. Roger van der Weyden, Portrait of Guillaume Fillastre; Maidenhead, Sir Thomas Ralph Merton Coll.

361. Roger van der Weyden, Portrait of a Man in Prayer; New York, Metropolitan Museum.

Plate 221.

363. Roger van der Weyden, Isabella of Portugal Designated as the Persian Sibyl; New York,
John D. Rockefeller, Jr., Coll.

Plate 222.

364. Roger van der Weyden, Portrait of a Gentleman; Lugano, Thyssen Coll.

Plate 223.

365. Roger van der Weyden, *The Grand Bâtard de Bourgogne*; Brussels, Mus. Royal.

Plate 224.

366. Roger van der Weyden, Francesco d'Este; New York, Metropolitan Museum.

Plate 225.

367. Roger van der Weyden, Portrait of a Young Lady; Washington, National Gallery.

Plate 226.

369. Roger van der Weyden (and Assistant), Jean Gros; Chicago, Art Institute.

368. Roger van der Weyden (Workshop), Madonna; Formerly Bruges, Renders Coll.

Plate 227.

371. Roger van der Weyden, Philippe de Croy; Antwerp, Mus. Royal.

370. Roger van der Weyden, Madonna; San Marino, Huntington Gall.

Plate 228.

373. Roger van der Weyden, Laurent Froimont; Brussels, Mus. Royal.

372. Roger van der Weyden, Madonna; Caen, Musée, Coll. Mancel.

Plate 229.

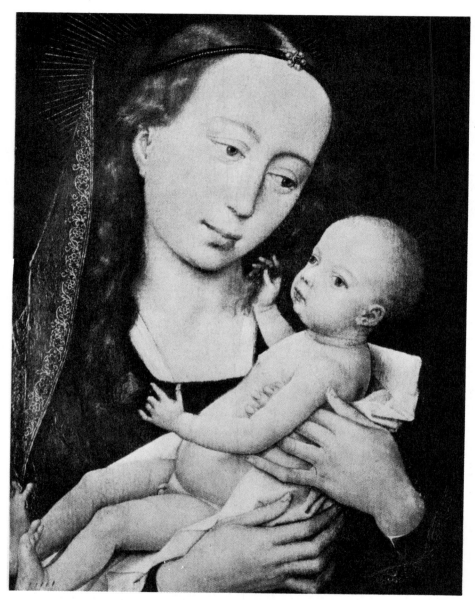

374. Roger van der Weyden, Madonna; Donaueschingen, Galerie.

Plate 230.

375. Roger van der Weyden, Madonna (Replica); Houston, Museum of Fine Arts (Straus Coll.).

Plate 231.

Plate 232.

379. Roger van der Weyden, Charles the bold (Replica); Berlin, Kaiser Friedrich Museum.

378. Roger van der Weyden (Workshop), John the Fearless, Antwerp, Mus. Royal.

Plate 233.

381. Roger van der Weyden (Workshop), Louis of Savoy (Silverpoint); Vierhouten, van Beuningen Coll.

380. Roger van der Weyden (Workshop), John of Brabant (Silverpoint); Vierhouten, van Beuningen Coll.

Plate 234.

383. Roger van der Weyden (Workshop), Philip of Nevers (Silverpoint);
Formerly Amsterdam, Mannheimer Coll. (Destroyed).

382. Roger van der Weyden (Workshop), Philip of Brabant (Silverpoint);
Formerly Amsterdam, Mannheimer Coll. (Destroyed).

Plate 235.

384. Roger van der Weyden (?), The Magdalen (Silverpoint); London, Brit. Mus.

Plate 236.

Plate 237.

387 a. Free Copy after Roger van der Weyden, Justice of Trajan and Herkinbald, Left Half (Tapestry); Berne, Historisches Museum.

Plate 238.

387 b. Free Copy after Roger van der Weyden, Justice of Trajan and Herkinbald, Right Half (Tapestry); Berne, Historisches Museum.

Plate 239.

389. Portrait of Roger van der Weyden; Arras, Abbaye de St.-Vaast, ms. 266.

388. Self-Portrait of Roger van der Weyden (Copy); Detail of fig. 387b.

Plate 240.

390. Roger van der Weyden (Workshop), Lamentation; Brussels, Mus. Royal.

Plate 241.

392. Copy after Roger van der Weyden, Bearing of the Body to the Sepulchre (Pen); Paris, Louvre.

391. Copy after Roger van der Weyden, Bearing of the Cross (Pen); Formerly Leipzig, Prof. F. Becker.

Plate 242.

393. Copy after Roger van der Weyden (Vrancke van der Stockt?), Descent from the Cross; Munich, Alte Pinakothek.

Plate 243.

395. Follower of Quentin Massys after Roger van der Weyden, Descent from the Cross; Madrid, Lazaro Coll.

394. Copy after Roger van der Weyden, Descent from the Cross; Nancy, Mus. Municipal.

Plate 244.

397. Follower of Roger van der Weyden, Exhumation of St. Hubert; London, National Gallery.

396. Follower of Roger van der Weyden, Dream of Pope Sergius; Haartekamp, Mme. von Pannwitz Coll.

Plate 245.

398. Follower of Roger van der Weyden, Calvary; Berlin, Kaiser Friedrich Museum.

Plate 246.

399. Follower of Roger van der Weyden, Triptych; Zug, Abegg Coll.

Plate 247.

Plate 248.

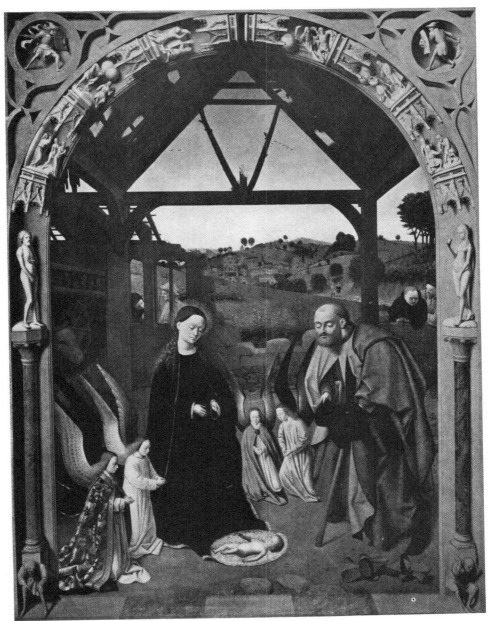

402. Petrus Christus, Nativity; Washington, National Gallery.

Plate 249.

403. Petrus Christus, Lamentation; Brussels, Mus. Royal.

Plate 250.

404. Petrus Christus, Lamentation; New York, Metropolitan Museum.

Plate 251.

405. Petrus Christus, Portrait of a Carthusian; New York, Metropolitan Museum.

Plate 252.

406. Petrus Christus, Edward Grymestone; Gorhambury, The Earl of Verulam (on loan to the National Gallery, London).

Plate 253.

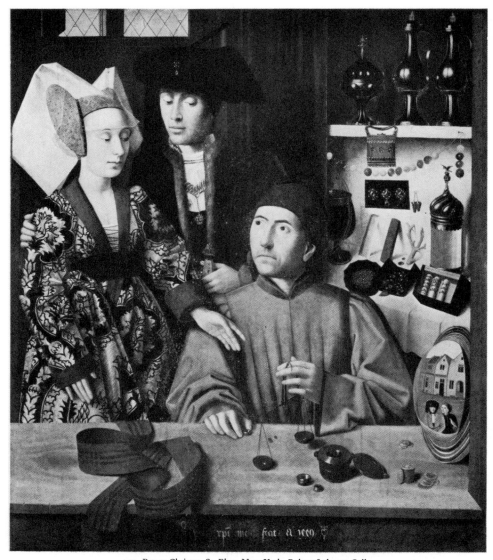

407. Petrus Christus, St. Eloy; New York, Robert Lehman Coll.

Plate 254.

408. Petrus Christus, Madonna of Jan Vos ("Exeter Madonna"); Berlin, Kaiser Friedrich Museum.

Plate 255.

409. Petrus Christus, Annunciation and Nativity; Berlin,
Kaiser Friedrich Museum.

410. Petrus Christus, Last Judgment; Berlin,
Kaiser Friedrich Museum.

Plate 256.

411. Petrus Christus Nativity; New York, Mr. Georges Wildenstein (formerly H. Goldman Coll.).

Plate 257.

412. Petrus Christus, Madonna and Saints; Frankfort, Städelsches Kunstinstitut.

Plate 258.

413. Petrus Christus, Portrait of a Young Girl; Berlin, Kaiser Friedrich Museum.

Plate 259.

415. Dirc Bouts, Visitation; Madrid, Prado.

414. Dirc Bouts, Annunciation; Madrid, Prado.

Plate 260.

417. Dirc Bouts, Adoration of the Magi; Madrid, Prado.

416. Dirc Bouts, Nativity; Madrid, Prado.

Plate 261.

418. Dirc Bouts, Triptych; Granada, Capilla Real.

Plate 262.

419. Dirc Bouts, Descent from the Cross; Central Panel of fig. 418.

Plate 263.

420. Dirc Bouts, Entombment; London, National Gallery.

Plate 264.

421. Dirc Bouts, Lamentation (Replica); Paris, Louvre.

Plate 265.

422. Dirc Bouts, Portrait of a Young Man; London, National Gallery.

Plate 266.

424. Copy after Petrus Christus, Portrait of a Falconer (Silverpoint); Frankfort, Städelsches Kunstinstitut.

423. Follower of Dirc Bouts, Self-Portrait (Silverpoint); Northampton, Smith College, Tryon Art Gall.

Plate 267.

425. Dirc Bouts, Madonna; New York, Metropolitan Museum.

Plate 268.

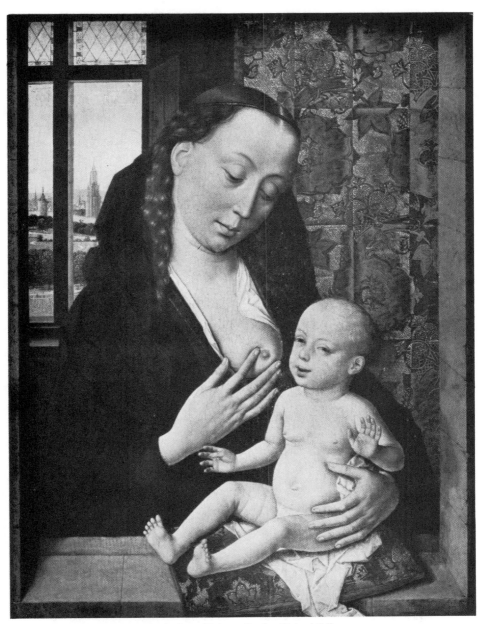

426. Dirc Bouts, Madonna; London, National Gallery.

Plate 269.

427. Dirc Bouts, Triptych; Louvain, St. Peter's.

Plate 270.

428. Dirc Bouts, Last Supper; Central Panel of Fig. 427.

Plate 271.

429. Dirc Bouts, Elijah in the Desert; Upper Right (?) Wing of fig. 427.

Plate 272.

430. Dirc Bouts, Gathering of Manna; Lower Left (?) Wing of fig. 427.

Plate 273.

431. Dirc Bouts, Wrongful Execution of the Count; Brussels, Mus. Royal.

Plate 274.

432. Dirc Bouts, Ordeal of the Countess; Brussels, Mus. Royal.

Plate 275.

433. Follower of Dirc Bouts, Adoration of the Magi (cf. fig. 434); Munich, Alte Pinakothek.

Plate 276.

434. Follower of Dirc Bouts, St. John the Baptist and St. Christopher; Wings of fig. 433.

Plate 277.

435. Albert van Ouwater, Raising of Lazarus; Berlin, Kaiser Friedrich Museum.

Plate 278.

436. Albert van Ouwater; Detail of fig. 435.

Plate 279.

437. Utrecht Master of *ca.* 1460, Triptych; Utrecht, Centraal Museum.

Plate 280.

438. Master of the Virgin Among Virgins, Lamentation; Liverpool, Walker Art Gallery.

Plate 281.

439. Geertgen tot Sint Jans, Holy Kinship, Amsterdam, Rijksmuseum.

Plate 282.

441. Geertgen tot Sint Jans, Madonna; Milan, Ambrosiana.

440. Geertgen tot Sint Jans; Detail of fig. 439.

Plate 283.

442. Geertgen tot Sint Jans, Raising of Lazarus; Paris, Louvre.

Plate 284.

443. Geertgen tot Sint Jans, St. John in the Wilderness; Berlin, Kaiser Friedrich Museum.

Plate 285.

444. Geertgen tot Sint Jans, Lamentation; Vienna, Gemäldegalerie.

Plate 286.

445. Geertgen tot Sint Jans, Story of the Remains of St. John the Baptist; Vienna, Gemäldegalerie.

Plate 287.

446. Geertgen tot Sint Jans; Detail of fig. 443.

Plate 288.

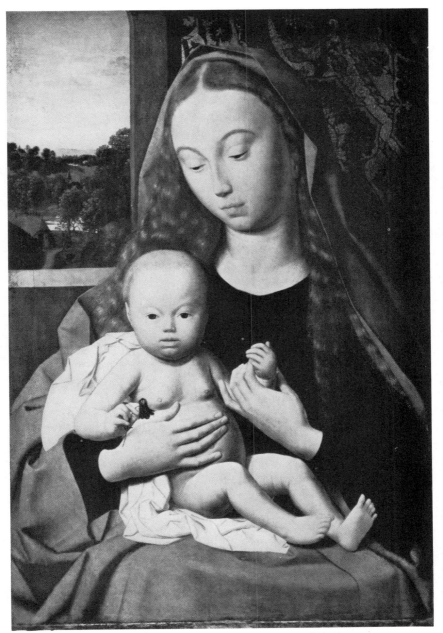

447. Geertgen tot Sint Jans, Madonna; Berlin, Kaiser Friedrich Museum.

Plate 289.

448. Geertgen tot Sint Jans, Nativity; London, National Gallery.

Plate 290.

449. Geertgen tot Sint Jans, Man of Sorrows; Utrecht, Archiepiscopal Museum

Plate 291.

450. Joos van Ghent, Adoration of the Magi; New York, Metropolitan Museum.

Plate 292.

451. Joos van Ghent, Triptych; Ghent, St. Bavo's.

Plate 293.

452. Joos van Ghent, Calvary; Central Panel of fig. 451.

Plate 294.

453. Joos van Ghent; Details of fig. 451.

Plate 295.

454. Joos van Ghent, Communion of the Apostles; Urbino, Palazzo Ducale.

Plate 296.

455. Hugo van der Goes and Follower, Triptych; Frankfort, Städelsches Kunstinstitut.

Plate 297.

456. Hugo van der Goes, Fall of Man; Vienna, Gemäldegalerie.

Plate 298.

457. Hugo van der Goes, Lamentation; Vienna, Gemäldegalerie.

Plate 299.

SANCTA · ŒNOVEFA·

458. Hugo van der Goes, St. Geneviève; Vienna, Gemäldegalerie.

Plate 300.

459. Hugo van der Goes, The "Monforte Altarpiece"; Berlin, Kaiser Friedrich Museum.

Plate 301.

460. Hugo van der Goes; Detail of fig. 459.

Plate 302.

461. Hugo van der Goes, The Portinari Altarpiece, Exterior; Florence, Uffizi.

Plate 303.

462. Hugo van der Goes, The Portinari Altarpiece, Interior; Florence, Uffizi.

Plate 304.

463. Hugo van der Goes, Nativity; Central Panel of fig. 462.

Plate 305.

464. Hugo van der Goes, Donors and Patron Saints; Wings of fig. 462.

Plate 306.

465. Hugo van der Goes, The Annunciate; Detail of fig. 461.

Plate 307.

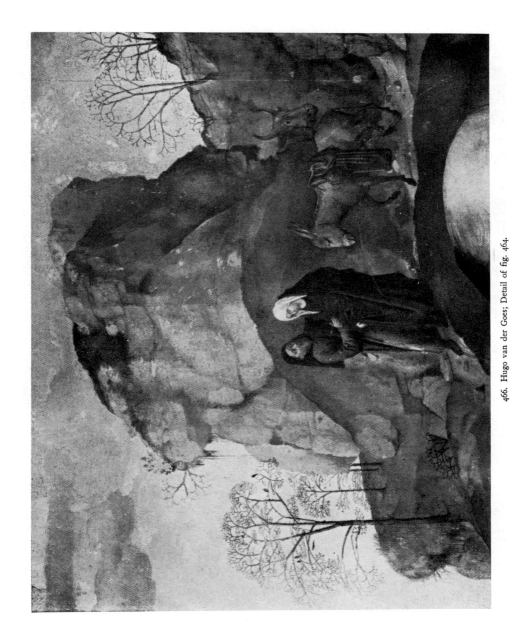

466. Hugo van der Goes; Detail of fig. 464.

Plate 308.

467. Hugo van der Goes and Followers, James III and Margaret of Scotland; Holyrood Palace
(on loan to the National Gallery of Scotland).

Plate 309.

468. Hugo van der Goes, Sir Edward Bonkil Venerating the Trinity; Holyrood Palace
(on loan to the National Gallery of Scotland).

Plate 310.

Plate 311.

471. Hugo van der Goes, Nativity; Berlin, Kaiser Friedrich Museum.

Plate 312.

472. Hugo van der Goes; Detail of fig. 471.

Plate 313.

473. Hugo van der Goes, Death of the Virgin; Bruges, Mus. Communal.

474. Follower of Hugo van der Goes, Adoration of the Magi;
Vienna, Liechtenstein Gallery.

475. Follower of Hugo van der Goes, Nativity;
Wilton House, The Earl of Pembroke.

Plate 315.

476. Hans Memlinc, The Donne of Kidwelly Altarpiece; Chatsworth, Chatsworth Estates Company.

Plate 316.

477. Hans Memlinc, Portrait of a Young
Fiancée; New York, Metropolitan Museum.

478. Hans Memlinc, Two Horses; Vierhouten,
van Beuningen Coll.

Plate 317.

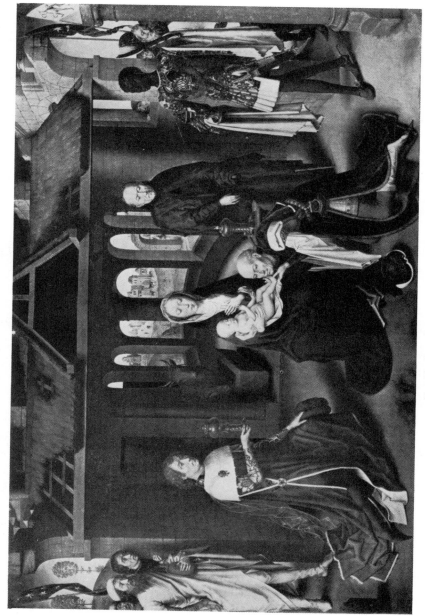

479. Hans Memlinc, Adoration of the Magi; Madrid, Prado.

Plate 318.

480. Hans Memlinc, Portrait of a Young Italian; Antwerp, Mus. Royal.

Plate 319.

481. Hans Memlinc, Madonna; Washington, National Gallery.

Plate 320.

482. Gerard David, The Lord Blessing; Paris, Louvre.

Plate 321.

483. Gerard David, Triptych; Paris, Louvre.

Plate 322.

484. Gerard David, The Virgin among Virgins; Rouen, Mus. de la Ville.

Plate 323.

485. Gerard David, Betrothal of St. Catherine; London, National Gallery.

Plate 324.

486. Gerard David, St. Catherine; Detail of fig. 485.

Plate 325.

487. Jan Gossart, Madonna in a Church; Rome, Galleria Doria.

Plate 326.

488. Jan Gossart, Deësis; Madrid, Prado.

Plate 327.

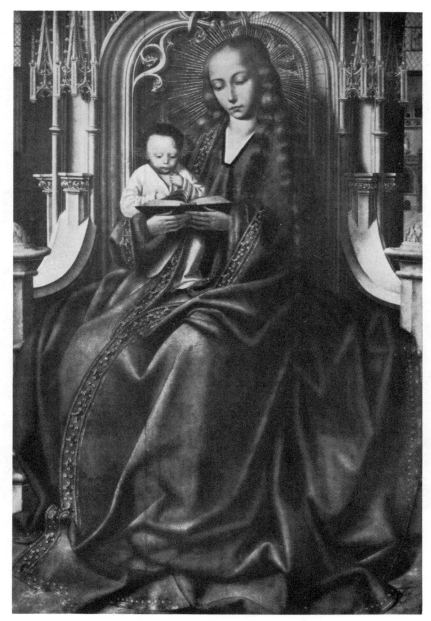

489. Quentin Massys, Madonna; Brussels, Mus. Royal.

Plate 328.

490. Quentin Massys, Madonna; London, Count A. Seilern Coll.

Plate 329.

491. Quentin Massys, The Money Changer and His Wife; Paris, Louvre.

Plate 330.

492. Quentin Massys, Portrait of an Elderly Man; Paris, Mus. Jacquemart-André.

Plate 331.

493. Quentin Massys, "The Ugly Duchess"; London, National Gallery.

Plate 332.

495. Master of the Death of the Virgin (Joos van Cleve?), Holy Family (Replica); New York, Metropolitan Museum.

494. Master of the Death of the Virgin (Joos van Cleve?), Holy Family; New York, Metropolitan Museum.

Plate 333.

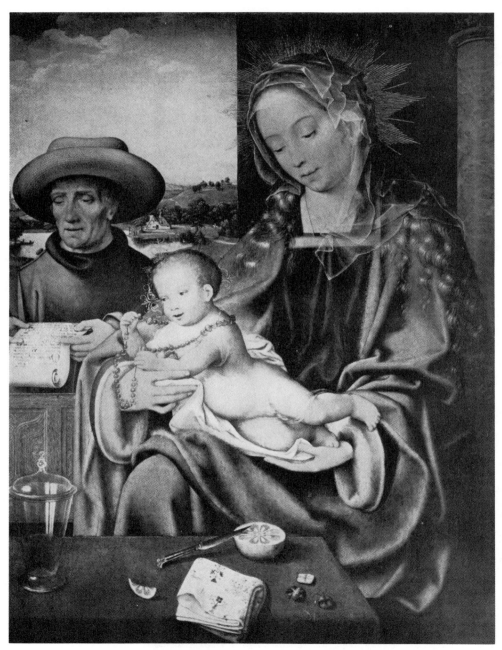

496. Master of the Death of the Virgin (Joos van Cleve?), Holy Family; Lugano, Thyssen Coll.

Plate 334.

Icon Editions